CROWN FINANCIAL MI

BIBLICAL
FINANCIAL
STUDY

SMALL GROUP

LEADER'S

GUIDE

TABLE OF CONTENTS

SUBJECT	PAGES
Course Objectives / Leader's Responsibilities	4
Information Leaders Need to Know	5-6
Student Orientation	7
Prayer Log	8
Loving the Students	9
How to Select and Train Leaders	10
How to Conduct the Study	11
How to Begin CROWN in the Church	12
Leader's Checklist	13
Places to Serve	14
Leader's Weekly Homework Guides	15-84
Leader's Evaluation and Suggestions, Student Evaluation, Care Log, and Prayer Logs	85-96

WEB SITE

CROWN has designed a Web site as a resource to provide students with up-to-date financial information, helpful articles, additional biblical insights, links to other useful Web sites, and much more. Visit the Web site at **www.crown.org** for a world of information.

CROWN'S MISSION STATEMENT

*Teaching people God's financial principles
in order to know Christ more intimately
and to be free to serve Him.*

Course Objectives/Leader's Responsibilities

OBJECTIVES OF THE STUDY

1. Encourage people to experience more intimate fellowship with Christ.
Luke 16:11 expresses the correlation between how we handle our resources and the quality of our fellowship with the Lord: *"Therefore if you have not been faithful in the use of worldly* wealth, who will entrust the true riches to you?"*

2. Challenge each person to invite Jesus Christ to be his or her Lord.
We believe money is the primary competitor with Christ for the lordship of our lives. Jesus said, *"No man can serve two masters, you will love one and hate the other. . . . You cannot serve God and Mammon [money]"* (Matthew 6:24).

3. Build close relationships among the participants.

4. Help students put their financial house in order.

THE PRIMARY RESPONSIBILITIES OF THE LEADER

1. Unconditionally love and encourage your students.
People are more receptive to spiritual truth when they have been loved. People want to know how much you care before they care how much you know.

2. Hold your students accountable.

3. Be a model of faithfulness.
In Luke 6:40 we read, *"Everyone, after he has been fully trained, will be like his teacher."* Leaders must be faithful to always arrive early, pray consistently for your students, know the memory verses fluently, and have your homework and practical applications prepared.

4. Conform to the CROWN FINANCIAL MINISTRIES' procedure of leading the study.

* The word *worldly* from the *New International Version* has been substituted for the word *unrighteous* from the *New American Standard Bible* to clarify the meaning of this passage.

1. The Leader's Guide

The *Leader's Guide* is divided into three sections:

- Information the leader needs to know
- The weekly homework guides
- The Prayer Logs, Care Log, and Student Evaluation.

2. Practical Application Video

Toward the end of class each week, you will play a segment of the *Practical Application Video*. There are 10 segments of the video—one for each week of the study. For example, at the end of Week 4, play segment 4 of the video.

The *Practical Application Video* explains the next week's assignment and communicates other important information the students need to know. After viewing the video, take time to answer any questions the students may have. Each small group should have a copy of the *Practical Application Video*.

3. Group Size

There should be two leaders in each group.

The maximum number of students in a group varies, depending on how many students are married couples and how many are individuals. Under no circumstance should there be more than **eight** students. We limit the size of the group because the group dynamic is damaged if the group is too large. The table below will assist you in determining your group size.

Leaders: Co-leaders:	Couple Couple	Couple/Single Couple/Single	Couple/Single Couple/Single	Couple/Single Couple/Single	Single Single
Students:	Couple Couple Couple Couple	Couple Couple Couple Single Single	Couple Couple Single Single Single	Couple Single Single Single Single	Single Single Single Single Single
Totals:	4 Leaders 8 Students	2-4 Leaders 8 Students	2-4 Leaders 7 Students	2-4 Leaders 6 Students	2 Leaders 5 Students

4. Meeting Time

The groups meet for two hours once each week for 10 weeks. The time and day the group meets should be the one most convenient for the participants. Groups may meet anywhere—in homes, offices, or churches. There are couples, men-only, women-only, and mixed groups.

5. Promoting Financial Products and Services

No one may use their affiliation with Crown Financial Ministries to promote or influence the sale of any investments or financial services or professional services.

6. Student Evaluation Sheet

The Student Evaluation Sheet is found on page 87 and should be used by the leader to record the performance of the students after each class.

7. Certificate of Achievement

The leaders should award the Certificate of Achievement to the students who have been faithful. They are provided free of charge, and they may be ordered online at **www.crown.org** or by calling 1-800-722-1976.

8. Scheduling the Study

The study is usually conducted three times each year, starting mid-January, the first part of May, and mid-September. However, you may begin a CROWN group anytime.

9. More About CROWN FINANCIAL MINISTRIES

What is CROWN FINANCIAL MINISTRIES? CROWN is an interdenominational ministry that has developed a comprehensive program to train people of all ages to apply the financial principles from the Bible.

Why is the ministry named CROWN? The reason this ministry is named CROWN is to remind us to always honor the Lord and serve people.

■ CROWN FINANCIAL MINISTRIES exists to glorify Jesus Christ. He wore a Crown of Thorns when, out of unfathomable love, He died for us (John 19:1-5). Just as the 24 elders in Revelation 4:9-11 cast their crowns before the throne of God, so those serving with CROWN should honor Christ in all that we do.

■ CROWN FINANCIAL MINISTRIES exists to serve people. Paul wrote to the Philippians, "*My beloved brothers whom I long to see, my joy and crown*" (Philippians 4:1).

Financial Information: CROWN FINANCIAL MINISTRIES is a nonprofit, tax-exempt organization governed by a board of directors, none of whom receive a salary from serving on the CROWN board. Book royalties are the property of the ministry. CROWN is a member of the Evangelical Council for Financial Accountability, whose members must adhere to certain standards, including an annual audit. The ministry is funded primarily by donations, the bulk of which come from graduates of CROWN studies, radio listeners, or churches that are implementing CROWN.

As the group is being assembled, the leaders should diligently **pray** that the Lord will bring just the right students into the group. Then the leaders should meet with their students as a group at least **two weeks** before the study begins. This Student Orientation may be done just with the members of your small group or there may be a church-wide or citywide orientation.

1. Start to love the students and build relationships.

2. Review the students' requirements by viewing the Student Orientation video.

It is located on the *Leader's Training Video*.

The requirements are designed to take approximately two hours each week outside of class. If for any reason someone comes to the class unprepared, that person will not be allowed to participate in the discussion. The student requirements:

- Daily homework
- Scripture to memorize each week
- Weekly practical application
- Daily prayer for each participant
- Attend eight of the 10 classes.

3. Observe the other important "ground rules."

- The class opens and closes in prayer.
- Scriptures are memorized in the version used in the CROWN materials and not in another version of the Bible.
- The classes start and stop on time.
- Group discussions are confidential.
- Students are trained to be future leaders by each person leading one of the weekly meetings.
- No one will be embarrassed by being required to expose his or her financial situation.

4. Dispense the materials and collect payment.

One student set is required for each person or married couple. A student set for couples contains two *Student Manuals*. A student set for an individual contains one *Student Manual*. Collect payment from the class.

5. Complete the Personal Information Sheet.

Ask each student to complete the Personal Information Sheet found on page 5 in the *Practical Application Workbook* and send it to CROWN. This is a self-addressed, postage-paid form that does not require an envelope. The Personal Information Sheets may be completed online by visiting **www.crown.org/piform.asp**. Crown wants to provide the students with helpful resources and continued education.

6. Assign the Week 1 homework.

The assignment is found on page 8 of the *Student Manual* and should be completed prior to attending Week 1. The assignment is to read *Your Money Counts*, memorize Luke 16:11, and answer the homework questions. Ask the students to bring their calendars to the first class to schedule the two socials.

PRAYER LOG

To help the participants develop a more consistent prayer life, we utilize the Prayer Log. During the first meeting, ask each person or couple to provide the small group information at the top of the Prayer Log: name and personal information.

- One Prayer Log should be filled out for each person or couple.
- End each class by taking prayer requests from each member or couple. The requests need not be limited to financial concerns. Prior to taking requests, inquire if they have experienced any answers to their prayer requests. There may be more than one request per week.
- To save time, ask the participants to complete their own Prayer Logs before coming to class. Each member is required to pray daily for every member in the group during the 10 weeks. Examine the sample Prayer Log below.

"Pray for one another" (JAMES 5:16).

Name **Don Norman** Spouse **Janet**

Home phone **321-2525** Children (ages) **Matthew (12)**

Buisness phone **542-1378** **Danielle (6)**

E-mail **djnorman@wayout.net**

Home address **272 Nelsen Ave**

Little Rock AR 72212

Week	Prayer Request(s)	Answers to Prayer
1	Matthew's cold to get better Don's relationship with boss improve	
2	Don's relationship with boss improve Janet's neighbor come to know Christ	Matthew is completely well
3	Our family faithful in applying God's financial principles	Don's relationship with his boss has improved
4	Our family to get out of debt Danielle to have good time at school	
5		

PRAYER LOG

1. Love your students outside of class.

Care Log. The purpose of the Care Log is to ensure that the leaders contact their students each week to encourage and love them. The weekly contacts may be by telephone, mail, e-mail, or in person. The two leaders should alternate each week in their responsibility to contact the students by deciding who will contact students on the odd-numbered weeks and who will contact the students on the even-numbered weeks.

The students should not be aware of the Care Log. The leaders should inspect each other's Care Logs weekly to encourage faithfulness.

CARE LOG

Leaders: **John Cole and Tim Manor**

Beginning Date of Small Group Study: **January 12, 2001**

WEEK	Initials of leader responsible for contact	Student(s) B. Hunt	Student(s) Mr. T Turner Mrs. B Turner	Student(s) J. Morgan	Student(s) G. Jones	Student(s)	Student(s)
1	JC	Phone 1/13	Lunch 1/14	Phone 1/14	Postcard 1/15		
2	TM	Phone 1/20	Phone 1/21	Wrote 1/20	Saw in person		
3	JC						
4	TM						

Socials. The leaders should organize two social events for the students. These activities may be for a dessert, a meal, or any other relaxed setting that will encourage the development of relationships. The first social should be scheduled midway through the study. The second social should be held as soon as possible after the study. It is also a good idea to visit the students where they work or live.

2. Love your students inside of class.

The leader's attitude should be loving, humble, and caring—not a critical or a know-it-all attitude. We are students-among-students; we all are growing in understanding the unfathomable Word of God.

After a student answers a question, encourage, affirm, and thank that student. If an answer is incorrect, be careful not to discourage the student by responding harshly or negatively. Maintain good eye contact and be attentive because we communicate through our body language.

HOW TO CONDUCT THE STUDY

1. Open with prayer. We recommend that you pray on your knees.

2. Individually recite the Scripture to memorize.

3. Confirm that the Practical Applications have been completed.

4. Conduct the group discussion. The discussion should proceed as follows.

   ▪ Different group members read the Scriptures for a particular day's homework.
   ▪ Proceed in a circle, asking every person to answer all the questions for that day's homework. If the answer to a question is obvious, it is not necessary for more than one person to answer the question.
   ▪ In a couples group, everyone should answer the Day One Homework. Then the men and women should alternate in answering the questions for Days Two through Six Homework.

5. Complete the items listed in the Remaining Agenda in consecutive order.

6. View the *Practical Application Video*.

7. Share prayer requests and write them in the Prayer Logs.

8. End in prayer.

SMALL GROUP DYNAMICS

▪ In Diagram 1 the sole focus is on the leader who does all the talking. The students are passive. This is not how CROWN is designed.
▪ Diagram 2 reflects a group interacting with one another and a leader who guides and facilitates the discussion. The leader must establish an environment in which students have the freedom to express their insights and questions.

DIAGRAM 1
The Wrong Method

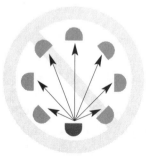

LEADER

DIAGRAM 2
The Correct Method

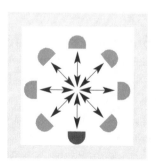

LEADER

How to Select and Train Leaders from Among Your Students

1. Set the Stage

In the student orientation, tell your students that you are going to train them to be leaders. Whether they become leaders depends on their desire to lead the study and their faithfulness during the study.

2. Test your Students

The most experienced leader should lead weeks one and two. The co-leader should lead weeks three and four. Then each student should be invited to lead one or two of the weeks.

3. Selection of Leaders

You should consider only the students who are faithful during the study.

4. Validation of Leaders

Any potential leader should be approved by the church leadership if the study is conducted within a church.

5. Invitation of Leaders

After a person has been selected and validated as a leader, invite that person to lead the study. If he or she decides to become a leader, that person needs to be trained.

6. Training of Leaders

For your students to be qualified to lead the study, they should do the following.

- Study the *Leader's Guide.*
- Complete a training session during which they view the *Leader's Training Video.* This training session may be conducted by a church or in a city-wide event, or it may be self-study, using the CD-ROM.

An explanation of how to begin CROWN in a church is described in detail in the *Church Manual*. The following is an abbreviated outline of the steps.

1. **Introduce** CROWN FINANCIAL MINISTRIES **to the pastor/church leadership.**
   Meet with the pastor and appropriate church leadership to explain the program. The *Introducing Crown Financial Ministries to the Church Leadership* video is very helpful in describing the program. These videos are located on the *Leader's Training Video*. To successfully implement the study in a church, it is essential to have the active support of the church leadership.

2. **Select and train the small group leaders.**
   The number of people that will need to be trained is determined by the number of groups the church wants to begin.

3. **Select the students for the initial group or groups.**
   The major objectives of the initial groups are to multiply the number of people qualified to lead and to enable some of the church leadership to experience the study.

4. **Choose the church initial coordinator.**
   The church coordinator (usually a layperson) has the overall responsibility of implementing CROWN FINANCIAL MINISTRIES within the church. This position requires a commitment of time and effort and should be the person's primary, if not sole, ministry. The pastor should be involved in the selection process. The first person serving in this role is often gifted as an initiator but will want to be replaced in a year or two.

5. **When CROWN is opened to the church.**
   - Bathe every presentation in prayer, asking the Lord to motivate the students He wants in the study.
   - Communicate the content and benefits of the study, and never use any hard-sell tactics. Describe the requirements and accountability and the need to invest two hours of preparation each week outside of class.
   - Churches have used several methods to present the study: a CROWN graduate's personal recommendation to a friend, the pastor's recommendation from the pulpit, testimonies from CROWN graduates in front of the church, an announcement in the church bulletin, and using the *Introducing Crown to Potential Small Group Students* video. This video is located on the *Leader's Training Video*.

There are four elements a leader must put in place to build a successful small group study.

1. The leader must love the students.
2. The leader must hold the students accountable.
3. The leader must model faithfulness.
4. The leader must conduct the study according to the CROWN FINANCIAL MINISTRIES procedure.

We want to serve you and help you maintain a standard of excellence. In order to assist you, an experienced CROWN small group leader may visit your group. After the class has ended and the students have departed, the experienced leader will meet with you to discuss the class and answer any questions. This is the checklist that will be used as a guide.

---

1. Describe how the leaders loved the students.

2. Did the leaders hold the students accountable to fulfill their responsibilities?

☐ Scripture Memory   ☐ Practical Application

☐ Homework   ☐ Daily Prayer

3. Did the leaders model faithfulness in the following areas?

☐ Scripture Memory   ☐ Practical Application

☐ Homework   ☐ Daily Prayer

☐ Student Evaluation Sheet   ☐ Care Log/Two Socials Scheduled

4. Did the leaders conduct the study according to the CROWN FINANCIAL MINISTRIES agenda?

☐ Start on Time   ☐ Correctly Lead Discussion

☐ Opening Prayer   ☐ View *Practical Application Video*

☐ Scripture Memory   ☐ Prayer Requests

☐ Confirm Practical Application   ☐ Ending Prayer / Stop on Time

Additional Comments:

PLACES TO SERVE

If you have a desire to help others learn God's way of handling money, there are four places you can serve with CROWN as illustrated in the baseball diamond.

1. **Serving Individuals.** The heroes of CROWN FINANCIAL MINISTRIES are the small group leaders and budget counselors, because the small group and one-on-one are where life changes take place.
2. **Serving the Church.** If you want to impact your entire church, you may serve as the church coordinator or on the church team.
3. **Serving Your City.** If you have a desire to influence your community, third base is for those who serve as a city director or on the city team. And in order for CROWN to have a broad impact on a larger city, it is necessary to have a full-time city director and a functioning team of volunteers.
4. **Serving Beyond the City.** Home plate is for those who have a "missionary spirit" and wish to help introduce CROWN to other cities and even other countries. If you wish to serve your church, or your city, or even beyond your city, visit CROWN's Web site at **www.crown.org/jobs.asp** for more information on these positions.

THE NEXT STEP

1. **What I need to do to begin my first group:**

   - My leader or co-leader is

   - My potential students are
     (Concentrate on selecting students who have the potential to become future small group leaders. It is also helpful to have someone representing the church leadership participate.)

   - Describe how you will ask the students to participate.

   - Describe how you will schedule the Student Orientation.

   - My goal is to start my first group by this date:

2. **What I need to do to help CROWN grow in my church:**

   - Meet with my pastor/church leadership to discuss CROWN FINANCIAL MINISTRIES.

   - The acting CROWN church coordinator is

   - Those who will serve on the initial church team are

INTRODUCTION

How We Handle Money Impacts Our Relationship with the Lord

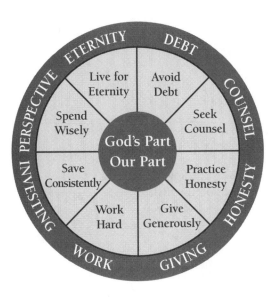

CROWN'S OVERVIEW OF WEEK 1: The primary objectives for Week 1 are to begin to develop close relationships among the participants and reinforce the study requirements. Leaders should read the Introduction Notes prior to attending class.

NOTE: The blank space following each agenda number is for the leader to fill in the scheduled time for each agenda item. For example, if your class begins at 7:00, #1 would read at 7:00, #2 would read at 7:05, #3 would read at 7:10, and so forth. This is designed to assist the leader in monitoring the time so that the class will end punctually.

AGENDA

1. _____ (5 minutes) **Open in prayer.**

2. _____ (5 minutes) **Each person individually recites from memory Luke 16:11.**

    "Therefore if you have not been faithful in the use of worldly* wealth, who will entrust the true riches to you?"

3. _____ (5 minutes) **Ask the students if they have filled out and mailed (or completed online) the Personal Information Sheet found on page 5 of the *Practical Application Workbook*. Review the requirements found on page 4 of the *Student Manual*.**

4. _____ (70 minutes) **Ask everyone to introduce themselves, beginning with a leader. Ask them to share how they were introduced to Jesus Christ, what they do for a living, and something about their families. To determine how much time each person is allotted, divide the number of people into 70 minutes. The leaders should communicate this time constraint. If a student is too brief, the leader should gently ask additional questions to provide the student with an opportunity to express himself or herself more fully.**

5. _____ (10 minutes) **Begin the homework discussion.**

* The word *worldly* from the New International Version has been substituted for the word *unrighteous* from the New American Standard Version to clarify the meaning of this passage.

1. What was the most helpful information you learned from reading *Your Money Counts*?

Read *Isaiah 55:8-9*.

2. Based on this passage, do you think God's financial principles will differ from how most people handle money? What do you think would be the greatest difference?

> **NOTE TO LEADER:** CROWN'S comments, enclosed in brackets, will follow each question. Following CROWN'S comments there will be space for the leader's response to the question.

[God's economy operates on entirely different principles. Most people do not believe the Lord plays a role in finances, but Scripture reveals He has the dominant role].

Read *Luke 16:11*.

3. What does this verse communicate to you about the importance of managing possessions faithfully?

[How we handle money affects our fellowship with Christ.]

4. How does handling money impact our fellowship with the Lord?

[If we are unfaithful with money, our fellowship with the Lord will suffer.]

Scripture memory helps: The memory verses are found in the back of the *Practical Application Workbook* and are designed to be removed and carried with you throughout the day. The verses have been set to music and are on the CD at the end of the *Practical Application Workbook*.

INTRODUCTION

REMAINING AGENDA

1. _____ (5 minutes) **Play the Week 1 segment of the *Practical Application Video,* which reviews what the students are required to do for next week.**

   - Read the Introduction Notes on pages 10 and 11 in the *Student Manual.*

   - Complete the God's Part/Our Part Homework on pages 14 to 19 in the *Student Manual.*

   - Begin recording Income and Spending, complete the Personal Financial Statement, and prepare the Quit Claim Deed on pages 7 to 17 in the *Practical Application Workbook.*

2. _____ (5 minutes) **After viewing the Week 1 segment of the *Practical Application Video,* answer any questions the students have about next week's assignment.**

   - **REVIEW THE CALENDAR** to determine if any regularly scheduled classes fall on a holiday. If there are any conflicts, please reschedule at this meeting.

   - **SCHEDULE THE TWO SOCIALS.**

   - **COMPLETE THE PRAYER LOGS.** Participants should have one Prayer Log for each person or couple, including himself or herself.

3. _____ (10 minutes) **Take prayer requests and note them in the Prayer Log.**

4. _____ (5 minutes) **End in prayer.**

REMINDER FOR LEADERS: Complete the students' evaluations on page 87. Decide which leader will be responsible for what week on the Care Log. Be sure to contact each student this week. Encourage students who have not already done so to complete the Personal Information Sheets and send them to CROWN FINANCIAL MINISTRIES (or complete them online).

GOD'S PART/OUR PART

Lord Is Owner of All

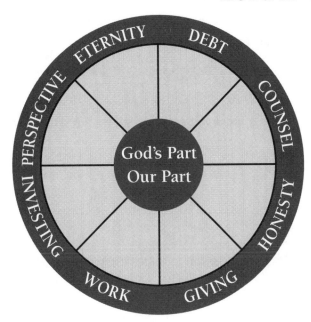

REMINDER FOR LEADERS: Complete the students' evaluations. Decide which leader will be responsible for what week on the Care Log. Be sure to contact each student this week. Continue to encourage students to complete their Personal Information Sheets and send them to CROWN FINANCIAL MINISTRIES.

AGENDA

1. _____ (5 minutes) **Open in prayer.**

2. _____ (5 minutes) **Each person individually recites from memory 1 Chronicles 29:11-12, TLB.**

   "Everything in the heavens and earth is yours, O Lord, and this is your kingdom. We adore you as being in control of everything. Riches and honor come from you alone, and you are the Ruler of all mankind; your hand controls power and might, and it is at your discretion that men are made great and given strength."

3. _____ (5 minutes) **Confirm that everyone has completed the Personal Financial Statement practical application, has started the Recording Income and Spending worksheet, has completed the Quit Claim Deed, and has reviewed the Financial Goals samples. Ask the students to have their completed deeds witnessed by others in the group. Answer any questions concerning the practical applications.**

4. _____ (80 minutes) **Begin the group discussion.**

DAY ONE

Read the Introduction Notes on pages 10 and 11 and answer.

LEADERS—The participants should read the Notes before class, not during the class.

1. What information especially interested you?

   [Emphasize that how we handle money affects our fellowship with Christ.]

2. Comment on any personal challenges you felt after learning the three reasons the Bible says so much about money.

DAY TWO

Read *Deuteronomy 10:14*; *Psalm 24:1*; and *1 Corinthians 10:26* and answer.

1. What do these passages teach about the ownership of your possessions?

   [The Lord owns everything in the world.]

GOD'S PART/OUR PART

Read *Leviticus 25:23; Psalm 50:10-12;* and *Haggai 2:8.*

2. What are some of the specific items that the Lord owns?

> *Leviticus 25:23*—**[God owns all the land.]**

> *Psalm 50:10-12*—**[God owns all the animals.]**

> *Haggai 2:8*—**[God owns all the gold and silver.]**

3. Prayerfully evaluate your attitude of ownership toward your possessions. Do you consistently recognize the true owner of those possessions? Give two practical suggestions to help recognize God's ownership.

   [Consider altering your vocabulary by dropping the possessive pronouns ("my," "mine," and "ours") and substituting "His" or "the" instead. For 30 days, each morning and night, meditate and prayerfully recite 1 Chronicles 29:11-12.]

   ■

   ■

Read *1 Chronicles 29:11-12* and *Psalm 135:6.*

1. What do these verses say about the Lord's control of circumstances?

   [**The Lord is in control of all circumstances.**]

Read *Proverbs 21:1; Isaiah 40:21-24;* and *Acts 17:26.*

2. What do these passages tell you about the Lord's control of people?

   Proverbs 21:1—[**God controls the heart of each person.**]

   Isaiah 40:21-24—[**The Lord is in absolute control of all people.**]

   Acts 17:26—[**The Lord controls the boundaries and duration of every nation.**]

3. Do you normally recognize the Lord's control of all events? If not, how can you become more consistent in recognizing His control?

LEADER—you should have approximately **one hour** of class time remaining. We recommend a three-minute stretch break for your group at this time.

GOD'S PART/OUR PART

DAY FOUR

Read *Genesis 45:4-8; Genesis 50:19-20;* and *Romans 8:28.*

1. Why is it important to realize that God controls and uses even difficult circumstances for good in the life a godly person?

   [God works every circumstance for good in the life of those who love Him and are yielded to Him as Lord. Joseph suffered difficult circumstances, but God orchestrated those difficulties for ultimate good.]

2. How does this perspective impact you today?

3. Share a difficult circumstance you have experienced and how the Lord ultimately used it for good in your life.

DAY FIVE

Read *Psalm 34:9-10; Matthew 6:31-33;* and *Philippians 4:19.*

1. What has the Lord promised about meeting your needs?

   [God has promised to provide our needs if we seek first the kingdom of God and His righteousness.]

2. From the Bible, give an example of the Lord providing for someone's needs in a supernatural way.

[Several of the many examples of God's provision: Israel in the wilderness (Exodus 16:4-35), Jesus feeding the five thousand (Matthew 14:15-21) and the four thousand (Matthew 15:32-38), and the Lord sending ravens to feed Elijah (1 Kings 17:4-6).]

3. How does this apply to you today?

[The Lord continues to provide for us today.]

DAY SIX

Read *1 Corinthians 4:2.*

1. According to this verse what is your requirement as a steward?

[We are responsible to be faithful as stewards.]

2. How would you define a steward?

[A steward is a manager of another's property.]

Read *Luke 16:1-2.*

3. Why did the master remove the steward from his position?

[The steward was removed because he squandered the master's possessions.]

Read *Luke 16:10*.

4. Describe the principle found in this verse.

   [If a person is unfaithful in a little matter, he or she will be unfaithful in much, and vice versa.]

5. How does this apply in your situation?

REMAINING AGENDA

1. _____ (10 minutes) **Play the Week 2 segment of the *Practical Application Video,* which reviews what the students are required to do for next week. Answer any questions concerning the practical application.**

   - Read the God's Part/Our Part Notes on pages 20 to 28 in the *Student Manual*.
   - Complete the Debt Homework on pages 30 to 33 in the *Student Manual*.
   - Complete the Debt List and Debt Repayment Schedule on pages 23 to 30 in the *Practical Application Workbook*.

2. _____ (10 minutes) **Note requests and answers to prayer in the Prayer Log.**

3. _____ (5 minutes) **End in prayer.**

REMINDER FOR LEADERS: Remember to be vulnerable with your own financial challenges. Contact each student this week and record the communication in the Care Log on page 88. Please review the mechanics of How to Conduct the Study on page 11 to confirm that you are conducting the discussion correctly.

Leader's Guide for Week 3

DEBT
Debt Is Slavery

CROWN'S OVERVIEW OF WEEK 3: Debt is a struggle for many and is discouraged in Scripture. This week challenge the students to establish the goal of becoming debt free. Prior to attending class, the leader should read the Debt Notes on pages 34-45 of the Student Manual.

AGENDA:

1. _____ (5 minutes) **Open in prayer.**

2. _____ (5 minutes) **Each person individually recites from memory Proverbs 22:7, TLB.**

   "Just as the rich rule the poor, so the borrower is servant to the lender."

3. _____ (5 minutes) **Confirm that everyone has completed the practical applications of the Debt List and the Debt Repayment Schedule. Answer any questions concerning the practical applications.**

4. _____ (80 minutes) **Begin the group discussion.**

DAY ONE

Read the God's Part/Our Part Notes on pages 20 to 28 of the Student Manual.

1. How have you observed the Lord using money to mold your character?

2. What strengths have been developed in your character?

3. What weaknesses in your character still need to be addressed?

DAY TWO

Read *Deuteronomy 15:4-6; Deuteronomy 28:1,2,12;* **and** *Deuteronomy 28:15,43-45.*

1. According to these passages, how was debt viewed in the Old Testament?
   [Debt was considered a curse. Being free from debt (being a lender) was a blessing.]

2. What was the cause of someone getting in debt (becoming a borrower) or getting out of debt (becoming a lender)?
   [Disobedience led to debt and obedience led to getting out of debt (being a lender).]

Read *Romans 13:8; Proverbs 22:7;* **and** *1 Corinthians 7:23.*

1. Is debt encouraged in Scripture? Why?

    Romans 13:8—[**We are encouraged to stay out of debt.**]

    Proverbs 22:7—[**The debtor is servant to the lender.**]

    1 Corinthians 7:23—[**We are instructed not to be slaves of men. Therefore, make every effort to get out and stay out of debt. To summarize: the Bible does not say that debt is sin, but it discourages indebtedness.**]

2. How does this apply to you personally and to your business?

3. If you are in debt, do you have a strategy to get out of debt? If you have a plan, please describe it.

DEBT

DAY FOUR

Read *Psalm 37:21* and *Proverbs 3:27-28.*

1. What do these verses say about debt repayment?

    Psalm 37:21—[**A person who borrows but does not repay debts is called** *wicked.*]

    Proverbs 3:27-28—[**Pay debts promptly if you have the resources. Many are taught to delay repayment to use other people's money as long as possible, but this is not biblical.**]

2. How will you implement this?

DAY FIVE

Read 2 *Kings 4:1-7.*

1. What principles of getting out of debt can you identify from this passage?

[**We should seek the counsel of godly people, as well as the Lord's help and direction. His supernatural intervention is required whether He answers quickly, as in the case of the widow, or more slowly over time. We should use whatever resources are available—however small—in an effort to get out of debt. Involve the entire family in your effort to get out of debt.**]

2. Can you apply any of these principles to your present situation? How?

Read *Proverbs 22:26-27* and *Proverbs 17:18.*

1. What does the Bible say about cosigning (striking hands, surety)?

    Proverbs 22:26-27—[**Do not cosign. It may cause you to lose assets you need.**]

    Proverbs 17:18—[**It is poor judgment to cosign (countersign).**]

Read *Proverbs 6:1-5.*

2. If someone has cosigned, what should he or she attempt to do?

    [**If we have cosigned, we are to humbly and diligently seek the release of our obligation.**]

REMAINING AGENDA

1. _____ (10 minutes) **Play the Week 3 segment of the *Practical Application Video*, which reviews what the students are required to do for next week. Answer any questions concerning the practical applications.**

    ■ Read the Debt Notes on pages 34 to 45 in the *Student Manual.*

    ■ Complete the Counsel Homework on pages 48 to 53 in the *Student Manual.*

    ■ Complete the Estimated Budget on pages 31 to 37 in the *Practical Application Workbook.*

2. _____ (10 minutes) **Note requests and answers to prayer in the Prayer Logs.**

3. _____ (5 minutes) **End in prayer.**

REMINDER FOR LEADERS: In order to more consistently recognize God's ownership, encourage your students to continue meditating on *1 Chronicles 29:11-12.* Contact each student this week and note this in the Care Log. Remind the students to visit Crown's Web site at **www.crown.org** for more practical assistance in getting out of debt.

DEBT

COUNSEL

A Wise Person Seeks Advice

CROWN'S OVERVIEW OF WEEK 4: Everyone should seek counsel when they need to make major financial decisions. In our culture people are discouraged from seeking counsel. The leader should read the Counsel Notes prior to attending class.

AGENDA

1. _____ (5 minutes) **Open in prayer.**

2. _____ (5 minutes) **Each person individually recites from memory Proverbs 12:15.**

   "The way of a fool is right in his own eyes, but a wise man is he who listens to counsel."

3. _____ (5 minutes) **Confirm that everyone has completed the practical application of the Estimated Budget. Answer any questions concerning the practical applications.**

4. _____ (80 minutes) **Begin the group discussion.**

Read the Debt Notes on pages 34 to 45 in the Student Manual.

1. Are you in debt? If so, what steps do you sense the Lord wants you to take to become free of debt? If not, what safeguards do you have in place to help you remain debt free?

   [Encourage your students to work toward getting out of debt.]

2. What did you learn about debt that proved to be especially helpful?

DAY TWO

Read *Proverbs 12:15; Proverbs 13:10;* and *Proverbs 15:22.*

1. What are some of the benefits of seeking counsel?

   Proverbs 12:15—[**The person who listens to counsel is wise.**]

   Proverbs 13:10—[**Wisdom comes to those who seek counsel, but the consequence of not seeking counsel is strife.**]

   Proverbs 15:22—[**Plans succeed with counsel but fail without it.**]

2. What are some of the benefits you have experienced from seeking counsel?

3. What hinders you from seeking counsel?

DAY THREE

Read *Psalm 16:7* and *Psalm 32:8*.

1. Does the Lord actively counsel His children? How?

[**The Lord does counsel His children primarily through prayer, the Bible, and godly people.**]

Read *Psalm 106:13-15*.

2. What was the consequence of not seeking the Lord's counsel in this passage?

[**A *wasting disease* was sent because they did not seek the counsel of the Lord.**]

3. Have you ever suffered for not seeking the Lord's counsel? If so, describe what happened.

LEADER — you should have approximately **one hour** of class time remaining. We recommend a three-minute stretch break for your group at this time.

DAY FOUR

Read *Psalm 119:24*; *Psalm 119:105*; *2 Timothy 3:16-17*; and *Hebrews 4:12*.

1. Should the Bible also serve as your counselor? Why?

[**We must seek the counsel of the Word of God because it gives direction for our lives.**]

Read *Psalm 119:98-100.*

2. Living by the counsel of Scripture—

■ Makes us wiser than: **[Our enemies]**

■ Gives us more insight than: **[Our teachers]**

■ Gives us more understanding than: **[Those older and more experienced]**

3. Do you consistently read and study the Bible? If not, what prevents your consistency?

DAY FIVE

Read *Proverbs 1:8-9.*

1. Who should be among your counselors?

[Our parents should be among our counselors.]

2. In your opinion, who should be the number one human counselor of a husband? Of a wife? Why?

[The husband and wife are each other's most important human counselor.]

Read *Proverbs 11:14* and *Ecclesiastes 4:9-12*.

3. What do these verses communicate to you?

Proverbs 11:14—[**People fail without counsel, but many counselors lead to victory.**]

Ecclesiastes 4:9-12—[**Two or three people working together are more productive than a single individual.**]

4. How do you propose to apply this principle in your personal and/or business life?

DAY SIX

Read *Psalm 1:1-3*.

1. Whom should you avoid as a counselor?

[**Avoid the wicked as your counselor.**]

2. What is your definition of a wicked person?

[**A wicked person is one who lives his or her life without regard to God.**]

Read *Proverbs 12:5.*

3. Why should you avoid that counsel?

[**The thoughts of the wicked are not controlled by the Holy Spirit and are deceitful.**]

4. Is there ever a circumstance in which you should seek the input of a person who does not know Christ? If so, when?

[**In our opinion, it is permissible to seek input from those who do not know Christ when you are gathering facts. After collecting the facts, solicit counsel from godly people before arriving at your decision.**]

REMAINING AGENDA

1. _____ (10 minutes) **Play the Week 4 segment of the *Practical Application Video,* which reviews what the students are required to do for next week. Answer any questions concerning the practical applications.**

   ▪ Read the Counsel Notes on pages 54 to 61 in the *Student Manual.*

   ▪ Complete the Honesty Homework on pages 64 to 68 in the *Student Manual.*

   ▪ Complete Adjusting Your Budget on pages 39 to 44 in the *Practical Application Workbook.*

2. _____ (10 minutes) **Note in the Prayer Logs requests and answers to prayer.**

3. _____ (5 minutes) **End in prayer.**

REMINDER FOR LEADERS: Remember to complete the students' evaluations.

COUNSEL

HONESTY

CROWN'S OVERVIEW OF WEEK 5: Dishonest practices are common, but the Lord demands that His children act with absolute honesty and integrity. This section is one of the most challenging of the entire study. The leader should read the Honesty Notes prior to attending class.

AGENDA:

1. _____ (5 minutes) **Open in prayer.**

2. _____ (5 minutes) **Each person individually recites from memory Leviticus 19:11.**
   "You shall not steal, nor deal falsely, nor lie to one another."

3. _____ (5 minutes) **Confirm that everyone has completed the Adjusting Your Budget practical application. Answer any questions concerning the practical applications.**

4. _____ (80 minutes) **Begin the group discussion.**

Read the Counsel Notes on page 54 to 61.

1. What elements of God's perspective of counsel especially interested you?

   [Encourage married couples to seek counsel from their spouses.]

2. Do you actively seek counsel when faced with a major financial decision? If not, how do you propose to do so in the future?

DAY TWO

Read *Leviticus 19:11-13; Deuteronomy 25:13-16; Ephesians 4:25;* **and** *1 Peter 1:15-16.*

1. What do these verses communicate to you about God's demand for honesty?

   Leviticus 19:11-13—**[The Lord commands us to be honest.]**

   Deuteronomy 25:13-16—**[The Lord demands honesty in our business dealings.]**

   Ephesians 4:25—**[We are not to lie to one another.]**

   1 Peter 1:15-16—**[We are to be holy in our behavior just as the Lord is holy.]**

2. Are you consistently honest in even the smallest details? If not, what will you do to change?

3. What are two factors that motivate or influence us to act dishonestly?

   [**Some of the factors influencing dishonesty are greed, fearing that God will not provide for us, financial difficulties, and peer pressure.**]

   ■

   ■

4. How does this apply to you?

DAY THREE

Read *Exodus 18:21-22*.

1. Does the Lord require honesty for leaders? Why?

   [**The Lord requires leaders to be honest. A major criteria for selecting leadership was honesty, because a leader will influence those under his or her authority, either for good or for evil.**]

Then read *Proverbs 28:16* **and** *Proverbs 29:12.*

2. What are the consequences of dishonesty for people in leadership?

> *Proverbs 28:16*—[**A dishonest person will be removed from leadership.**]

> *Proverbs 29:12*—[**Subordinates will become dishonest.**]

3. How does this apply to you?

LEADER—you should have approximately **one hour** of class time remaining. We recommend a three-minute stretch break for your group at this time.

DAY FOUR

Read *Proverbs 14:2.*

1. Can you practice dishonesty and still love God? Why?

[**No, those who practice dishonesty despise the Lord. When people are dishonest, they have concluded that God is not able to provide exactly what they need, incapable of discovering their dishonesty, and powerless to discipline them. In short, dishonest people act as if the Lord does not exist.**]

Read *Proverbs 26:28* **and** *Romans 13:9-10.*

2. According to these passages, can you practice dishonesty and still love your neighbor? Why?

[**No, because dishonest people hate those they hurt. However, love does no wrong to a neighbor. Because dishonesty always affects people, we cannot love and be dishonest at the same time.**]

Read *Psalm 15:1-5; Proverbs 12:22; Proverbs 20:7;* and *Isaiah 33:15-16.*

1. What are some of the benefits of honesty?

Psalm 15:1-5—[**More intimate fellowship with the Lord.**]

Proverbs 12:22—[**An honest person is a delight to the Lord.**]

Proverbs 20:7—[**The children of an honest person are blessed.**]

Isaiah 33:15-16—[**The Lord will protect and provide for the needs of the honest.**]

Read *Proverbs 3:32; Proverbs 13:11;* and *Proverbs 21:6.*

2. What are some of the curses of dishonesty?

Proverbs 3:32—[**A dishonest person is an abomination to the Lord.**]

Proverbs 13:11—[**Anything obtained dishonestly will be taken away.**]

HONESTY

Proverbs 21:6—[**Obtaining wealth by lying produces only temporary gains and eventually leads to death.**]

DAY SIX

Read *Exodus 22:1-4; Numbers 5:5-8;* and *Luke 19:8.*

1. What does the Bible say about restitution?

[**Restitution was required under the Old Testament law. Zaccheus is an example of a person fulfilling this obligation. Restitution involved the return of the item acquired dishonestly, plus a penalty.**]

2. If you have acquired anything dishonestly, how will you make restitution?

[**Ask forgiveness from the Lord, confess your dishonesty to the one who was harmed, and make restitution. Sometimes restitution is a delicate and complex issue. The question of how to fulfill the principle of restitution should be prayerfully answered.**]

Read *Exodus 23:8; Proverbs 15:27;* and *Proverbs 29:4.*

3. What does Scripture say about bribes?

[**You must never take a bribe, because it will influence your judgment. The person who is not involved with bribes will live, but a leader who takes bribes will be overthrown.**]

4. Have you ever been asked to give or take a bribe? If so, describe what happened.

REMAINING AGENDA

1. _____ (10 minutes) **Play the Week 5 segment of the *Practical Application Video,* which reviews what the students are required to do for next week. Answer any questions concerning the practical applications.**

    - Read the Honesty Notes on pages 69 to 78 in the *Student Manual.*

    - Complete the Giving Homework on pages 80 to 83 in the *Student Manual.*

    - Complete Beginning Your Budget on pages 45 to 83 in the *Practical Application Workbook.*

2. **Ask students to recommend and/or contact people who might be future students. Forward any recommendations to the CROWN church or city leader.**

3. _____ (10 minutes) **Note requests and answers to prayers in the Prayer Log.**

4. _____ (5 minutes) **End in prayer.**

REMINDER FOR LEADERS: Encourage those who do not yet have a current will to obtain one.

GIVING
Giving Is Blessed

CROWN'S OVERVIEW OF WEEK 6: Communicate the importance of giving with the proper attitude. The leaders should read the Giving Notes prior to attending class.

AGENDA

1. _____ (5 minutes) **Open in prayer.**

2. _____ (5 minutes) **Each individual recites from memory Acts 20:35.**

   "Remember the words of the Lord Jesus, that He Himself said, 'It is more blessed to give than to receive.'"

3. _____ (5 minutes) **Confirm that everyone has completed the Beginning Your Budget practical application, and check their progress in getting a will. Answer any questions concerning the practical applications.**

4. _____ (80 minutes) **Begin the group discussion.**

Read the Honesty Notes on pages 69 to 78.

1. How does the example of Abraham in *Genesis 14:21-23* challenge you to be honest?

   [**Abraham made a commitment to the Lord not to take even a thread or a sandal thong. We need to make a similar commitment to be honest, even in the smallest matters.**]

2. Ask the Lord to reveal any areas of dishonesty in your life. How do you propose to deal with these areas?

DAY TWO

Read *Matthew 23:23*; *1 Corinthians 13:3*; and *2 Corinthians 9:7*.

1. What do these passages communicate about the importance of the proper attitude in giving?

   Matthew 23:23 — [**The Pharisees gave precisely the correct amount—a tithe of even their mint leaves. But because they gave with the wrong heart attitude, the Lord rebuked them.**]

   1 Corinthians 13:3 — [**Giving without a heart of love is of no value to the giver.**]

   2 Corinthians 9:7 — [**Do not give grudgingly or under compulsion but rather give cheerfully. The proper attitude is crucial.**]

GIVING

2. How do you think a person can develop the proper attitude in giving?

[**The proper attitude is the key issue in the area of giving. The only way to give out of a heart of love is to consciously give each gift to Jesus Christ Himself as an act of worship.**]

3. How would you describe your attitude in giving?

DAY THREE

Read *Acts 20:35*.

1. How does this principle from God's economy differ from the way most people view giving?

[**In the Lord's economic system it is more blessed to give than to receive. Most people believe the opposite.**]

2. List the benefits for the giver that are found in each of the following passages.

Proverbs 11:24-25—[**There is a material increase—in the Lord's time and way—to the giver.**]

Matthew 6:20—[**We can lay up treasures in heaven that we will be able to enjoy through out all eternity.**]

GIVING

Luke 12:34—[**The heart of the giver is drawn to Christ as treasures are given to Him.**]

1 Timothy 6:18-19—[**We can store treasures in heaven and** *"take hold of that which is life indeed."*]

LEADER—you should have approximately **one hour** of class time remaining. We recommend a three-minute stretch break for your group at this time.

DAY FOUR

Read *Malachi 3:8-10.*

1. Was the tithe (giving ten percent) required under Old Testament Law?

[**The tithe was required under the law, and it was considered robbing God not to give these required gifts.**]

Read *2 Corinthians 8:1-5.*

2. Identify three principles from this passage that should influence how much you give.

[**They first gave themselves to the Lord, asking Him to direct their giving. In the same way we need to submit ourselves to the Lord when determining how much to give.**]

[**They were so yielded to the Lord that despite difficult circumstances they begged to give.**]

[**They experienced tremendous joy as a result of their sacrificial giving.**]

■

■

■

Prayerfully (with your spouse if you are married) seek the Lord's guidance to determine how much you should give. You will not be asked to disclose the amount.

DAY FIVE

Read *Numbers 18:8-10,24; Galatians 6:6*; and *1 Timothy 5:17-18.*

1. What do these verses tell you about financially supporting your church and those who teach the Scriptures?

   Numbers 18:8-10,24—[**Godly people have always been required to participate in the maintenance of the ministry. The Old Testament believer was required to care for the place of worship and the Levites who served in the ministry.**]

   Galatians 6:6—[**Those who are taught the Scriptures should financially support their teachers.**]

   1 Timothy 5:17-18—[**God's New Testament instrument is the church, and we are to adequately support those who serve as pastors and teachers.**]

Read *Isaiah 58:6-11* and *Ezekiel 16:49*.

1. What do these verses say about giving to the poor?

Isaiah 58:6-11—[**When we give to the poor, the Lord will protect us, answer our prayers, and bless us with His joy**].

Ezekiel 16:49—[**The primary sins of Sodom were pride and not caring for the poor, even though they had an abundance of material goods.**]

Read *Matthew 25:35-45*.

2. How does Jesus Christ identify with the needy?

[**Jesus identifies personally with the poor. When we give to the poor, we are giving to Christ Himself. When we do not give to the poor, we are not giving to Christ, and He is left hungry and naked.**]

Read *Galatians 2:9-10*.

3. What does this verse communicate to you about giving to the poor?

[**The disciples also had a deep concern for the poor. After Paul's confirmation to minister to the Gentiles, the only counsel the disciples gave him was not to forget the poor. Think of the many issues they could have discussed. Yet, they only asked Paul to remember the poor.**]

4. Are you currently giving to the needy? If not, what is hindering you?

[**If your students do not already have a needy person in their lives, encourage them to ask the Lord to bring one.**]

GIVING

REMAINING AGENDA

1. _____ (10 minutes) **Play the Week 6 segment of the *Practical Application Video,* which reviews what the students are required to do for next week. Answer any questions concerning the practical applications.**

   - Read the Giving Notes on pages 84 to 92 in the *Student Manual.*

   - Complete the Work Homework on pages 94 to 100 in the *Student Manual.*

   - Review the Checking Account and Budget Hints on page 85 to 88 in the *Practical Application Workbook.*

2. _____ (10 minutes) **Note requests and answers to prayers in the Prayer Log.**

3. _____ (5 minutes) **End in prayer.**

Leader's Guide for Week 7

WORK
Work Diligently As Unto the Lord

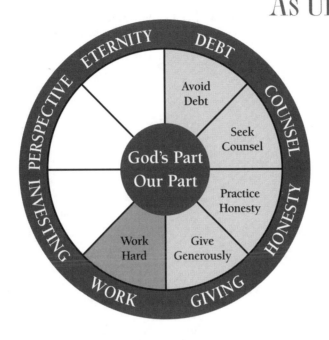

CROWN'S OVERVIEW OF WEEK 7: Work can be one of the most fulfilling or frustrating areas of life. Our satisfaction is dependent on understanding the Lord's perspective of work. The leader should read the Work Notes prior to attending class.

AGENDA:

1. _____ (5 minutes) **Open in prayer.**

2. _____ (5 minutes) **Everyone individually recites from memory Colossians 3:23-24.**

    "Whatever you do, do your work heartily, as for the Lord rather than for men. . . . It is the Lord Christ whom you serve."

3. _____ (5 minutes) **Confirm that everyone understands Your Checking Account practical application. Determine your students progress in obtaining a will. Answer any questions concerning the practical applications.**

4. _____ (80 minutes) **Begin the group discussion.**

NOTE: Please give your leader the name of anyone who would be interested in becoming a student in a future group.

DAY ONE

Read the Giving Notes on pages 84 to 92.

1. From God's perspective, it is important to give with the proper attitude. How will this influence your giving?

   [To be drawn more closely to the Lord and reap the other advantages intended for the giver, we need to give each gift to the person of Jesus Christ out of a grateful heart filled with love.]

2. What truth about giving did you learn that proved especially helpful? In what way?

DAY TWO

Read *Genesis 2:15*.

1. Why is it important to recognize that the Lord created work before sin entered the world?

   [Yes, work was instituted prior to sin entering the world. In the perfect, sinless environment of the Garden of Eden, God created work for our benefit. Work is not a result of sin and the curse.]

Read *Genesis 3:17-19*.

2. What was the consequence of sin on work?

   [Work became difficult as a result of sin.]

Read *Exodus 20:9* and *2 Thessalonians 3:10-12*.

3. What do these passages say to you about work?

Exodus 20:9—[**Old Testament believers were required to work six days each week.**]

2 Thessalonians 3:10-12—[**In the New Testament, work is also required. This verse does not recommend hunger for those who cannot work because of physical or mental limitations—only those who are capable of working but choose not to work.**]

DAY THREE

Read *Genesis 39:2-5; Exodus 35:30-35; Exodus 36:1-2;* and *Psalm 75:6-7*.

1. What do these verses tell us about the Lord's involvement in our work?

Genesis 39:2-5—[**The Lord is in control of success.**]

Exodus 35:30-35—[**The Lord gives us job skills and the ability to teach.**]

Exodus 36:1-2—[**The Lord gives us our skills and understanding.**]

Psalm 75:6-7—[**The Lord controls promotion and demotion.**]

WORK

2. How do these truths differ from the way most people view work?

[**The biblical perspective of God's part in work is in remarkable contradiction to the culture around us that does not acknowledge the Lord in work.**]

3. How will this perspective impact your work?

[**Our work attitudes and actions should be dramatically different from those who do not recognize God's role in work. We should be humble in any of our accomplishments because God gives us skills, success, and promotion.**]

LEADER—you should have approximately **one hour** of class time remaining. We recommend a three-minute stretch break for your group at this time.

DAY FOUR

Read *Ephesians 6:5-9; Colossians 3:22-25;* and *1 Peter 2:18.*

1. What responsibilities do the employer and employee have according to these verses?

Employee responsibilities:

[**Sincere obedience to employer—even one who is not good and gentle—work as unto the Lord; work heartily.**]

Employer responsibilities:

[**The employer should serve and not threaten employees.**]

2. For whom do you really work? How will this understanding change your work performance?

[**We work for the Lord. This perspective will allow us to make a sincere effort—even in difficult circumstances—to serve those who are our superiors or subordinates.**]

Read *Proverbs 6:6-11; Proverbs 18:9; and 2 Thessalonians 3:7-9.*

1. What does the Lord say about working hard?

> *Proverbs 6:6-11*—[**Ants are commended for hard work and those who are lazy are warned of poverty.**]

> *Proverbs 18:9* —[**A lazy person is compared to someone who destroys.**]

> *2 Thessalonians 3:7-9* —[**Paul modeled hard work.**]

2. Do you work hard? If not, describe what steps you will take to improve your work habits.

Read *Exodus 34:21.*

3. What does this verse communicate to you about rest?

> [**Hard work should be balanced with adequate rest and tempered by other biblical priorities. Even during busy times, one day of rest each week was required.**]

4. Do you get enough rest?

5. How do you guard against overwork?

WORK

Read *Proverbs 31:10-28* and *Titus 2:4-5*.

1. What do these passages tell us about women working?

> *Proverbs 31:10-28*—[**The excellent wife is diligent, works with her hands, acquires and prepares food, invests, provides clothes for the family, and sells merchandise. She works outside the home but always with a focus toward the home.**]

> *Titus 2:4-5*—[**Young wives were encouraged to be workers at home.**]

2. If you are a woman, how does this apply to your situation?

Read *2 Corinthians 6:14-18*.

3. How does this concept of "yoking" or "being bound together" apply to partnerships in business and work?

[**The principle of yoking applies to business partnerships. It is permissible for an employee to work for an employer who does not know Christ, but partnership with an unbeliever is discouraged.**]

4. Can you give some examples from the Bible of people who retired?

[**Scripture gives no example of people retiring and gives only one direct reference to retirement, which is found in *Numbers 8:24-26*. The instruction there applied exclusively to the Levites who had worked on the tabernacle.**]

WORK

5. Do you think retirement, as it is practiced in our culture, is biblically acceptable? Why or why not?

[Many people retire and cease all labor to pursue a life filled with leisure. This is not biblical. We should seek to be productive as long as we are able.]

REMAINING AGENDA

1. _____ (10 minutes) **Play the Week 7 segment of the *Practical Application Video*, which reviews what the students are required to do for next week. Answer any questions concerning the practical applications.**

   - Read the Work Notes on pages 101 to 111 in the *Student Manual*.

   - Complete the Investing Homework on pages 114 to 119 in the *Student Manual*.

   - Complete the Organizing Your Estate section on pages 89 to 93 of the *Practical Application Workbook*.

   Encourage your students to continue budgeting. Ask them to think of three creative ways to save money that would normally be spent. As the students share their ideas next week, this can be a powerful experience when they consider how steady savings grow over time.

2. _____ (10 minutes) **Note requests and answers to prayers in the Prayer Logs.**

3. _____ (5 minutes) **End in prayer.**

INVESTING
Consistently Save

CROWN'S OVERVIEW OF WEEK 8: This week's objectives are to learn the proper biblical attitudes toward saving and investing and to teach the scriptural framework for savings and investing. **The leaders should not recommend any specific investments or financial products or services.** CROWN FINANCIAL MINISTRIES assumes no liability for any actions taken related to specific investments or savings. The leaders should read the Investing Notes prior to attending class.

AGENDA

1. _____ (5 minutes) **Open in prayer.**

2. _____ (5 minutes) **Everyone individually recites from memory Proverbs 21:5.**

   "Steady plodding brings prosperity; hasty speculation brings poverty"
   (Proverbs 21:5, TLB).

3. _____ (5 minutes) **Confirm that everyone completed the Organizing Your Estate practical application and is continuing with their budgets. Answer any questions concerning the practical applications.**

4. _____ (10 minutes) **Ask the students to share their creative ideas on how to save money that would normally be spent.**

5. _____ (70 minutes) **Begin the group discussion.**

Read the Work Notes on pages 101 to 111.

1. What in the notes proved especially helpful or challenging? How will this impact you?

2. Do you usually recognize you are working for the Lord? If not, what can you do to be more aware that you work for the Lord?

Read *Genesis 41:34-36; Proverbs 21:20;* and *Proverbs 30:24-25*.

1. What do these passages say to you about savings?

Genesis 41:34-36 —[**Joseph saved during a time of plenty to prepare for a coming famine.**]

Proverbs 21:20 —[**Those who are wise save, but the foolish only consume.**]

Proverbs 30:24-25 —[**Ants are commended as wise because they save.**]

2. If you are not yet saving, how do you propose to begin?

Read *Luke 12:16-21,34.*

3. Why did the Lord call the rich man a fool?

[**The rich man was a fool because he stored up all his goods and was not rich toward God.**]

4. According to this parable, why do you think it is scripturally permissible to save only when you are also giving?

[**If we save without giving, our hearts will be drawn to those possessions and away from Christ (v. 34).**]

DAY THREE

Read *1 Timothy 5:8.*

1. What is a scripturally acceptable goal for saving?

[**It is permissible to save to meet family needs.**]

Read *1 Timothy 6:9.*

2. What is a scripturally unacceptable reason for saving?

[**It is wrong to desire to get rich. However, it is not wrong to become rich if it is a by-product of being a faithful steward.**]

Read *1 Timothy 6:10.*

3. According to this verse, why is it wrong to want to get rich (refer to *1 Timothy 6:9*)? Do you have the desire to get rich?

[**When we want to get rich we are actually loving money. The desire to get rich is a common attitude that can destroy our fellowship with the Lord.**]

Read *1 Timothy 6:11*.

4. What should you do if you have the desire to get rich?

   [**You should flee from this desire and pursue godly living.**]

LEADER—you should have approximately **one hour** of class time remaining. We recommend a three-minute stretch break for your group at this time.

DAY FOUR

Read *Proverbs 21:5; Proverbs 24:27; Proverbs 27:23-24; Ecclesiastes 3:1; Ecclesiastes 11:2; and Isaiah 48:17-18.*

1. What investment principle(s) can you learn from each of these verses, and how will you apply each principle to your life?

   Proverbs 21:5—[**Be a diligent, steady plodder and not hasty in investing.**]

   Proverbs 24:27—[**Develop your means of producing an income before buying a house.**]

   Proverbs 27:23-24—[**Know the status of your assets at all times.**]

   Ecclesiastes 3:1—[**Timing is important in investing.**]

Ecclesiastes 11:2—[**Diversify your investments.**]

Isaiah 48:17-18—[**The Lord teaches us to prosper, and we need to seek Him as we make investment decisions.**]

DAY FIVE

Read *Genesis 24:35-36; Proverbs 13:22;* **and** *2 Corinthians 12:14.*

1. Should parents attempt to leave a material inheritance to their children?

   [**Yes, parents should try to leave a material inheritance to their children.**]

2. How are you going to implement this principle?

Read *Proverbs 20:21* **and** *Galatians 4:1-2.*

3. What caution should a parent exercise?

   Proverbs 20:21—[**An inheritance should not be given into a child's care until the child is mature enough to manage the inheritance faithfully.**]

   Galatians 4:1-2—[**The appointment of a guardian through a will or trust helps ensure a child's maturity before receiving an inheritance.**]

INVESTING

Gambling is defined as *playing games of chance for money* and *betting*. Some of today's most common forms of gambling are casino wagering, betting on sporting events, horse and dog races, and state-run lotteries.

1. What are some of the motivations that cause people to gamble?

   [**People are motivated to gamble by the desire to get rich quick, by greed, and by the prospect of getting something for nothing. Many want to become wealthy so they can quit working.**]

2. Do these motives please the Lord? Why?

   [**These motives do not please the Lord because they are contrary to His principles found in the Bible.**]

Read *Proverbs 28:20* and *Proverbs 28:22*.

3. According to these passages, why do you think a godly person should not gamble (play lotteries, bet on sporting events)?

   [**A person who hastens after wealth is identified as evil and will experience poverty. Please encourage your students never to bet one penny. State lotteries are particularly enticing because they have been legalized by the government and glamorized by the media.**]

4. How does gambling contradict the scriptural principles of working diligently and being a faithful steward of the Lord's possessions?

   [**Gambling is in direct opposition to the scriptural principles of diligent work and faithful stewardship. No productive work is required in gambling; thus, a person's character is not properly developed. The odds of winning are absurdly low, and gamblers are wasting the possessions the Lord has entrusted to them.**]

REMAINING AGENDA

1. _____ (10 minutes) **Play the Week 8 segment of the *Practical Application Video,* which reviews what the students are required to do for next week. Answer any questions concerning the practical applications.**

   - Read the Investing Notes on pages 120 to 133 in the *Student Manual.*
   - Complete the Perspective Homework on pages 136 to 140 in the *Student Manual.*
   - Complete Organizing Your Insurance on pages 95 to 97 in the *Practical Application Workbook.*

2. _____ (10 minutes) **Note in the Prayer Log requests and answers to prayers.**

3. _____ (5 minutes) **End in prayer.**

REMINDER FOR LEADER: Please recommend the students who are qualified to be future leaders. Encourage those who do not yet have a current will to get one. Remind the students to visit CROWN's Web site at **www.crown.org** for much more practical information on investing.

PERSPECTIVE

CROWN'S OVERVIEW OF WEEK 9: This week we will determine our God-given standard of living. In many respects, this section is the summary of the entire study. The leader should read the Perspective Notes prior to attending class.

AGENDA:

1. _____ (5 minutes) **Open in prayer.**

2. _____ (5 minutes) **Everyone individually recites from memory Philippians 4:11-13.**

   "I have learned to be content in whatever circumstances I am. I know how to get along with humble means, and I also know how to live in prosperity. . . . I can do all things through Him who strengthens me."

3. _____ (5 minutes) **Confirm that everyone has completed the Organizing Your Insurance practical application and is budgeting faithfully. Determine the progress of the students' efforts to obtain a will. Answer any questions concerning the practical applications.**

4. _____ (80 minutes) **Begin the group discussion.**

   Note: Think about your prayer request for the last class. It should be a "long-term" request the others can pray about when they think of you.

DAY ONE

Read the Investing Notes on pages 120 to 133.

1. What in the notes proved especially helpful?

2. Carefully study the principle of compounding in the Investing Notes. Assume you earned 10 percent interest and saved $1,000 a year. Approximately how much would you accumulate by age 65 if you started saving today?

   $_____ *(refer to the graph on page 127 in the Investing Notes).*

3. Describe the specific steps you intend to take to begin saving.

DAY TWO

Read *Deuteronomy 30:15-16*; *Joshua 1:8*; and *Hebrews 11:36-40*.

1. What do each of these passages communicate to you about financial prosperity for the believer?

   Deuteronomy 30:15-16 —[**One of the blessings of obedience was prosperity.**]

   Joshua 1:8—[**Knowing and obeying all of the commands in the Scriptures resulted in prosperity.**]

   Hebrews 11:36-40—[**Even godly people have experienced poverty and difficult circumstances while exercising faith.**]

PERSPECTIVE

Reflect on the lives of Job (Job 1:3,13-22); Joseph (Genesis 37:26-28, 41:39-44); and Paul (Philippians 4:11-13).

2. Did they ever experience periods of financial abundance and at other times a lack of financial prosperity?

[**Job, Joseph, and Paul each experienced periods of plenty and times of want.**]

3. Was their lack of financial prosperity a result of sin or lack of faith?

[**Their times of poverty usually were not a result of sin or lack of faith.**]

4. Should all Christians always prosper financially? Why?

[**Once a person has fulfilled all areas of being a faithful steward, he or she is in a position for the Lord to prosper him or her financially. However, the Lord may not for one of three reasons: (1) He is building our character (*Romans 5:3-4*); (2) He needs to discipline us in areas of our lives where there is sin (*Hebrews 12:6,10*); and (3) God's sovereignty (*Hebrews 11:36-40*).**]

Read *Psalm 73:1-20*.

5. What does this passage tell you about the prosperity of the wicked?

[**The psalmist questioned why the wicked prospered. He was envious. Godliness did not seem to "pay off." Then the Lord revealed the wicked person's end: sudden, eternal punishment.**]

DAY THREE

Read *Philippians 4:11-13* and *1 Timothy 6:6-8*.

1. What do these passages say about contentment?

Philippians 4:11-13—[**Contentment is not something that occurs naturally; it is learned. We can learn to be content in any circumstance.**]

1 Timothy 6:6-8—[**Godliness with contentment is a means of great gain. We cannot take any thing with us when we die, and we should be content with our basic needs satisfied.**]

2. How does our culture discourage contentment?

3. How do you propose to practice contentment?

LEADER—you should have approximately **one hour** of class time remaining. We recommend a three-minute stretch break for your group at this time.

DAY FOUR

Read *Matthew 22:17-21* **and** *Romans 13:1-7*.

1. Does the Lord require us to pay taxes to the government? Why?

[**The Lord requires us to pay taxes because He has instituted government to serve people. The consequence of tax evasion is punishment.**]

Read *James 2:1-9*.

2. What does Scripture say about partiality (showing favoritism)?

[**Do not show favoritism to the wealthy. It is sin to be partial.**]

PERSPECTIVE

3. Are you guilty of partiality, based on a person's financial, educational, or social status?

Read *Romans 12:16* and *Philippians 2:3.*

4. How do you plan to overcome partiality?

   [**Be of the same mind toward each person and consider each person as more important than yourself.**]

DAY FIVE

Read *Acts 4:32-37* and *1 Thessalonians 4:11-12.*

1. What do these passages communicate to you about lifestyle?

   Acts 4:32-37—[**An equality of needs being met within the body of Christ led to revival.**]

   1 Thessalonians 4:11-12—[**We are encouraged to live quiet, industrious lives.**]

2. How do the following factors influence your present spending and lifestyle?

   ▪ Comparing your lifestyle with that of friends and other people—

   ▪ Television, magazines, catalogs, and other advertisements—

■ Your study of the Bible —

■ Your commitment to Christ and to things that are important to Him —

3. Do you sense that the Lord would have you to change your spending or your standard of living? If so, in what way?

Read *Deuteronomy 6:6-7; Proverbs 22:6;* and *Ephesians 6:4.*

1. According to these passages, who is responsible for teaching children how to handle money from a biblical perspective?

   [It is the responsibility of the parents. Introduce the concept of establishing a strategy for independence—the goal of having each child independently managing his or her finances (with the exception of food and housing) by the senior year in high school.]

2. Stop and reflect for a few minutes: Describe how well you were prepared to manage money when you first left home as a young person?

   [Most children leave home ill-equipped to manage money.]

3. Describe how you would propose to train children to

   ■ Budget—

▪ Give—

▪ Save—

▪ Spend wisely—

REMAINING AGENDA

1. _____ (5 minutes) **Play the Week 9 segment of the *Practical Application Video,* which reviews what the students are required to do for next week.**

   ▪ Read the Perspective Notes on pages 141 to 156 in the *Student Manual.*

   ▪ Complete the Eternity Homework for Week 10 on pages 158 to 162 in the *Student Manual.*

   ▪ Complete the Financial Goals practical application.

2. **Ask your students to be thinking about a "lifetime" or "long-term" prayer request for next week. Also ask each one to write a letter to his or her pastor, describing the benefits of the study, because this will encourage the church leadership.**

3. _____ (5 minutes) **Answer any questions concerning the practical applications.**

4. _____ (10 minutes) **Note in the Prayer Logs requests and answers to prayers.**

5. _____ (5 minutes) **End in prayer.**

REMINDER FOR LEADERS: Prepare the Certificates of Achievement for the students who have been faithful.

INSTRUCT YOUR STUDENTS to complete the Involvement and Suggestions sheet found on page 109 in the *Practical Application Workbook.* The input from the students is very important for the continued improvement of this study. Ask the students to complete both sides of the form, fold it, seal it, and drop it in a mailbox. The form is self-addressed and postage paid. The form may be completed online by visiting **www.crown.org/isform.asp.** As soon as CROWN receives the Involvement and Suggestions sheet, a gift will be sent to the student or couple as an expression of gratitude.

ETERNITY

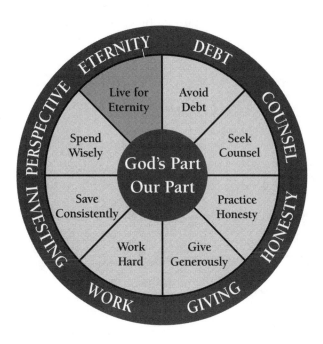

CROWN'S OVERVIEW OF WEEK 10: This section deals with God's view of our time on earth and eternity. To summarize, life on earth is short and eternity is forever. How we use our time, talents, and money will impact eternity.

AGENDA

1. _____ (5 minutes) **Open in prayer.**

2. _____ (5 minutes) **Everyone individually recites from memory Mark 8:36.**

   "What does it profit a man to gain the whole world, and forfeit his soul?"

3. _____ (5 minutes) **Confirm that everyone is continuing to budget and has executed a current will. Answer any questions concerning the practical applications.**

4. _____ (80 minutes) **Begin the group discussion.**

Read the Perspective Notes on pages 141 to 156.

1. What was the most helpful concept you learned from the notes?

2. Do you sense the Lord would have you alter your lifestyle in any way? If so, in what way?

DAY TWO

Read *Psalm 39:4-6* and *Psalm 103:13-16*.

1. What do these passages say to you about the length of life on earth?
   [**Life on earth is short.**]

Read *Psalm 90:10,12*.

2. Why do you think that Moses suggested numbering your days?
   [**Numbering our remaining days on earth helps us realize the brevity of our lives. Understanding this, we are better able to make wise decisions on how to use our time and money.**]

3. Estimate the number of days you have left on earth. How does this impact your thinking?

4. Based on your number of days, what actions will you take?

Read *1 Chronicles 29:15; Philippians 3:20;* and *1 Peter 2:11.*

1. What do these passages say about your identity on earth and in heaven?

   1 Chronicles 29:15—[**We are aliens, strangers, and sojourners on earth.**]

   Philippians 3:20—[**We are citizens of heaven, which is our real home.**]

   1 Peter 2:11—[**We are strangers on this earth.**]

Read *2 Peter 3:10-13.*

2. In the future what will happen to the earth?

   [**The earth and everything on it will be totally destroyed.**]

3. How should this impact the way you invest your time and spend money?

LEADER—you should have approximately **one hour** of class time remaining. We recommend a three-minute stretch break for your group at this time.

DAY FOUR

Read *Ecclesiastes 12:13-14* and *2 Corinthians 5:9-10.*

1. What will happen to each of us in the future?

   Ecclesiastes 12:13-14—[**The Lord will judge all our deeds, even those we think are hidden.**]

2 Corinthians 5:9-10—[**All of us will stand before the judgment seat of Christ and give an account of our actions.**]

Read *1 Corinthians 3:11-15.*

2. How would you describe the works (give some examples) that will be burned at this final judgment?

[**Any of our actions done out of what the Bible calls "the flesh"—apart from submission to Christ as Lord. Anything done out of pride or with improper motives.**]

3. Give some examples of works that will be rewarded.

[**The smallest action, when done to glorify Christ, will be rewarded. In** *Matthew 10:42* **the Lord tells us that even giving someone a cup of cold water shall be rewarded.**]

4. What are you doing that will survive this final judgment?

DAY FIVE

Read *2 Corinthians 4:18.*

1. What does this verse say to you?

[**What we see will last only a relatively short period of time. The things we cannot see will last forever and should be of primary importance.**]

2. As you reflect on eternity, answer thoughtfully: What three things do I want to accomplish during the rest of my life?

3. What can I do during my lifetime that would contribute most significantly to the cause of Christ?

4. In light of these answers, what actions or changes do I need to make?

DAY SIX

Read the Eternity Notes on pages 163 to 170.

1. What was the most important concept you learned from reading the notes?

2. Be sure you have read the Involvement and Suggestions sheet on page 109 in the *Practical Application Workbook*. Your opinion is important to us—so important that we have chosen to present a thank you gift to everyone who will take the few minutes necessary to fill out and return the sheet. Please fold and seal the completed sheet and drop it in the mail. Postage is prepaid. Or, if you prefer to complete the sheet online, go to www.crown.org/isform.asp. Please take a moment to complete the sheet *today*.

3. Describe what has been the most beneficial part of the Small Group Study for you.

REMAINING AGENDA

1. _____ (10 minutes) **Play the Week 10 segment of the *Practical Application Video*.**

2. _____ (5 minutes) **Award the Certificates of Achievement to those who successfully completed the course.**

3. _____ (5 minutes) **Take long-term prayer requests and note them on the Prayer Logs.**

4. _____ (5 minutes) **Leaders pray for each student individually.**

REMINDER FOR LEADERS: We suggest you write each member (or couple) an encouraging letter or e-mail, summarizing what you appreciate most about them. May the Lord richly bless you in every way for serving others.

LEADER'S EVALUATION AND SUGGESTIONS

CROWN wants to obtain your counsel The suggestions and insights of past participants have significantly improved the study. Please fill out both sides of this form. For your convenience, this form may be folded, sealed, and mailed to CROWN FINANCIAL MINISTRIES, postage paid (see the back of this form). To help save postage and processing costs, you may also complete this form online at **www.crown.org/lesform.asp**.

Please Print

YOUR NAME ☐ MR ☐ MRS ☐ MISS ☐ DR ☐ REV

HOME ADDRESS

CITY   ST/PROV   ZIP/POSTAL CODE

COUNTRY

E-MAIL ADDRESS

HOME PHONE   WORK PHONE

CHURCH NAME

CHURCH ADDRESS

CITY   ST/PROV   ZIP/POSTAL CODE

NEWSLETTER AND E-MAIL

We send a weekly e-mail message and monthly newsletter sharing God's principles and communicating what the Lord is doing in CROWN FINANCIAL MINISTRIES. Please indicate below if you would like to receive these.

☐ Yes, I would like to like to receive CROWN's weekly e-mail message.
☐ Yes, I would like to receive the monthly *Money Matters* newsletter.
☐ Yes, I would like to receive the monthly *Money Matters* newsletter by e-mail.

INVOLVEMENT

PRAY

☐ Yes, I would like to pray regularly for the Lord to expand CROWN and change lives through this ministry.

SUPPORT

☐ Enclosed is a contribution to CROWN in the amount of $_____.
☐ I want to become a regular supporter of CROWN (a CROWN Outreach Partner). Enclosed is my first contribution in the amount of $_____.

1. As a leader, please indicate the most significant impact of this study on your **students:**

    ❑ Prayed to receive Christ # _____
    ❑ Spiritual intimacy with God increased
    ❑ Debt reduced
    ❑ Savings increased
    ❑ Giving increased
    ❑ Marriages strengthened

    ❑ Relationships developed
    ❑ Time and service at church increased
    ❑ Accountability increased
    ❑ Leaders developed # _____
    ❑ Decisions for future spending
       were influenced.

    Additional comments:

    _____
    _____
    _____

2. Please share a brief testimony related to leading this study.

    _____
    _____
    _____
    _____
    _____
    _____

3. Do you have any practical hints that you would suggest to improve the study?

    _____
    _____
    _____

It is important to track the performance of your students to determine who is faithful. Place your students' names where indicated and place an "x" each week in the appropriate box when they have been faithful in their attendance, Scripture memory, practical application, or homework. Leave a box blank if they are not faithful in that particular area. Extra copies of this form may be printed from the CD-ROM in the back of this *Leader's Guide*.

WEEK ENDING	**Student Name ▶**					
	REQUIREMENTS					
1	ATTENDANCE					
	SCRIPTURE MEMORY					
	PRACTICAL APPLICATION					
	HOMEWORK					
2	ATTENDANCE					
	SCRIPTURE MEMORY					
	PRACTICAL APPLICATION					
	HOMEWORK					
3	ATTENDANCE					
	SCRIPTURE MEMORY					
	PRACTICAL APPLICATION					
	HOMEWORK					
4	ATTENDANCE					
	SCRIPTURE MEMORY					
	PRACTICAL APPLICATION					
	HOMEWORK					
5	ATTENDANCE					
	SCRIPTURE MEMORY					
	PRACTICAL APPLICATION					
	HOMEWORK					
6	ATTENDANCE					
	SCRIPTURE MEMORY					
	PRACTICAL APPLICATION					
	HOMEWORK					

WEEK ENDING					
7					
8					
9					
10					

CARE LOG

Leaders: _____

Beginning Date of Small Group Study: _____

WEEK	Initials of leader responsible for contact ♦	Student(s)	Student(s)	Student(s)	Student(s)	Student(s)	Student(s)
1							
2							
3							
4							
5							
6							
7							
8							
9							
10							

Description of first social activity (conduct about week five):

Description of second social activity (conduct about week 10):

PRAYER LOGS
Be Faithful in Prayer

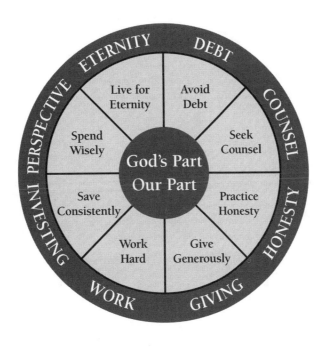

*"Pray for one another. . . . The effective prayer
of a righteous man can accomplish much"*
(James 5:16).

"Pray for one another" (JAMES 5:16).

Name _____   Spouse _____

Home phone _____   Children (ages) _____

Business phone _____   _____

E-mail _____   _____

Home address _____   _____

_____

WEEK	PRAYER REQUEST(S)	ANSWERS TO PRAYER
1		
2		
3		
4		
5		
6		
7		
8		
9		
10	My long term prayer request:	

PRAYER LOG

"Pray for one another" (JAMES 5:16).

Name _____ Spouse _____

Home phone _____ Children (ages) _____

Business phone _____ _____

E-mail _____ _____

Home address _____ _____

_____ _____

WEEK	PRAYER REQUEST(S)	ANSWERS TO PRAYER
1		
2		
3		
4		
5		
6		
7		
8		
9		
10	My long term prayer request:	

"Pray for one another" (JAMES 5:16).

Name _____ Spouse _____

Home phone _____ Children (ages) _____

Business phone _____ _____

E-mail _____ _____

Home address _____ _____

_____ _____

WEEK	PRAYER REQUEST(S)	ANSWERS TO PRAYER
1		
2		
3		
4		
5		
6		
7		
8		
9		
10	My long term prayer request:	

PRAYER LOG

"Pray for one another" (JAMES 5:16).

Name _____

Home phone _____

Business phone _____

E-mail _____

Home address _____

_____

Spouse _____

Children (ages) _____

_____

_____

_____

_____

WEEK	PRAYER REQUEST(S)	ANSWERS TO PRAYER
1		
2		
3		
4		
5		
6		
7		
8		
9		
10	My long term prayer request:	

PRAYER LOG

"Pray for one another" (JAMES 5:16).

Name _____   Spouse _____
Home phone _____   Children (ages) _____
Business phone _____   _____
E-mail _____   _____
Home address _____   _____
_____   _____

WEEK	PRAYER REQUEST(S)	ANSWERS TO PRAYER
1		
2		
3		
4		
5		
6		
7		
8		
9		
10	My long term prayer request:	

PRAYER LOG

"Pray for one another" (JAMES 5:16).

Name _____   Spouse _____
Home phone _____   Children (ages) _____
Business phone _____   _____
E-mail _____   _____
Home address _____   _____
_____   _____

WEEK	PRAYER REQUEST(S)	ANSWERS TO PRAYER
1		
2		
3		
4		
5		
6		
7		
8		
9		
10	My long term prayer request:	

"Pray for one another" (JAMES 5:16).

Name _____   Spouse _____

Home phone _____   Children (ages) _____

Business phone _____   _____

E-mail _____

Home address _____   _____

_____   _____

WEEK	PRAYER REQUEST(S)	ANSWERS TO PRAYER
1		
2		
3		
4		
5		
6		
7		
8		
9		
10	My long term prayer request:	

PRAYER LOG

OTHER PRODUCTS
FROM CROWN FINANCIAL MINISTRIES

is Bible study is full of
ivities to help make
rning basic financial prin-
les fun and exciting. It is
signed to be very "hands
" because children this age
rn from doing. The ABC's
ader's Guide offers the
cher a wide variety of
tional activities that rein-
ce the financial concepts in
ys that appeal to young chil-
en. Recommended for ages 7
d younger. Can be taught in a
all group setting, a Sunday school
ss, or one-on-one by a parent.

e ABC's of Handling Money God's Way
ll-color, 79 pages, hardcover)

ader's Guide
ll-color, 79 pages, softcover)

Four children with a
financial challenge learn
the secret of giving, saving, spending, and much
more. They also discover
that they can trust God to
provide. The principles
are embedded in a story
of adventure that captures
and holds the attention of
children. *The Secret* is in a
beautifully bound, hard-
cover Bible study with
color illustrations and makes
learning about money fun!
Recommended for ages 8-12.

The Secret
(Full-color, 103 pages, hardcover)

The Secret
(Black and white, 103 pages, softcover)

The Secret Leader's Guide
(88 pages, softcover)

ens love this Bible study!
sides memorizing key
riptures and learning what
od says about money, there
e also practical financial
ercises at the end of each
apter designed to help teens
eate habits that will set them
a lifelong journey of han-
ing money responsibly.

**scovering God's Way of Handling
oney for Teens Workbook** (156 pages, softcover)

**scovering God's Way of Handling
oney for Teens Leader's Guide** (104 pages, softcover)

College students are
facing growing finan-
cial challenges, such
as credit card debt
and even gambling.
The Crown Collegiate
*Biblical Financial
Study* is an excellent
study to teach God's
perspective of money
to students at the
formative time in their
lives.
Please call 1-800-722-1976 for more information on
how you can administer this study in your own local church
or classroom.

he *Career Direct—Youth Exploration Survey*® explores four areas:
rsonality, vocational interests, abilities, and priorities. It helps
udents apply survey results to their current activities and
lationships, and it points them toward an exciting future career.
ES! is fun, informative, interactive, and biblically based.

Career Direct YES!® Guidebook
(complete package, for individuals or groups)

Career Direct YES!® Leader's Guide
(88 pages, softcover—for youth pastors, guidance counselors, home school leaders)

My *Giving Bank* has
been designed to teach
your child the value of
money and how to han-
dle it in a way that is
pleasing to God. When
you order this 3-com-
partment bank made of
transparent blue plastic
from Crown, we also
include free, Bible-based
information for parents.

My Giving Bank
(For ages 3 and up, includes audio cassette and pamphlet)

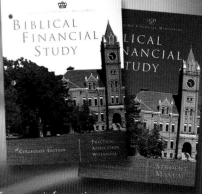
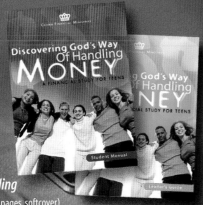

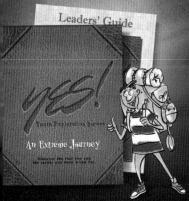
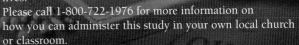

OTHER PRODUCTS
FROM CROWN FINANCIAL MINISTRIES

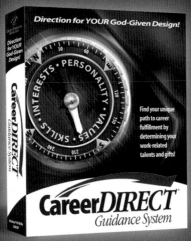

The fact is that people who enjoy what they are doing are more likely to succeed. The *Career Direct® Guidance System* on CD-ROM allows you to profile your personality, skills, interests, and values and instantly generates over 25 pages of individualized reports. It also comes with two excellent resource books and a series of audio messages to aid in educational and occupational decision making.

Money Matters 2005 is Crown's popular budgeting software that brings a fresh view to personal budgeting. The unique feature of this budgeting software package is its ability to hold the user accountable for each budgeting category. Plan, budget, and manage your family's finances with *Money Matters 2005!* (Free 30-day trial version available on the CD in the back of this workbook.)

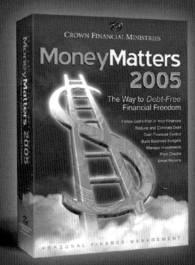

Career Direct Guidance System
(CD-ROM format, compatible with all Windows® PC platforms)

Money Matters 2005
(CD-ROM format, compatible with all Windows® PC platforms)

The *Budget Counselor Training Course* provides focused training for individuals who desire to become volunteer lay budget counselors. The textbook provides a foundation of biblical financial principles as well as practical helps to effectively counsel others. Join thousands who have chosen to help others become financially free to serve Him.

Budget Counselor Training Course
(Self-study course with books, audio, and software components)

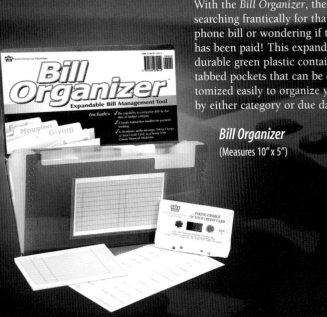

With the *Bill Organizer*, there's no more searching frantically for that misplaced phone bill or wondering if the power bill has been paid! This expanding file of durable green plastic contains 12 tabbed pockets that can be customized easily to organize your bills by either category or due date!

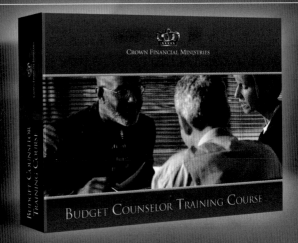

Bill Organizer
(Measures 10" x 5")

The *Cash Organizer* envelope budgeting system will simplify your budgeting process. Whether you are a beginning budgeter or need a handy tool for maintaining your budget, the *Cash Organizer* can help you. Twelve tear-resistant envelopes in a durable expanding file neatly divide your cash among budget categories. Preprinted stickers and a ledger booklet for tracking your income and expenses are included. And, each component of the *Cash Organizer* is translated into English and Spanish!

Cash Organizer
(Measures 4" x 7")

Visit us online at Crown.org for a complete listing of products and services, or call 1-800-722-1976 for a free materials catalog.